WHAT PEOPLE ARE SAYING ABOUT *KNOW CYBER RISK*:

*"**KNOW Cyber Risk** is a must read for all those managers that have IT systems supporting their business. Jim and Al have effectively introduced effective strategies on how to approach a security assessment and sell their bosses on security."*

— The Honorable Arthur L. Money, former Assistant Secretary of Defense for Command, Control, Communications and Intelligence, Department of Defense

"Entertaining, painless understanding of the need and advantages of conducting the dreaded computer and network security assessments. This will get managers wanting them."

— Ken Cutler, CISSP, CISA, Vice President, Information Security, MIS Training Institute

"Jim and Al have succeeded in demystifying the task of conducting an assessment. This book, written in an easy-to-read style, is full of strategies and tips on planning, conducting and dealing with the results of an assessment. I highly recommend it for anyone about to conduct an assessment."

— Charlie Baggett, CEO SAFEOperations, Inc.

"This book takes a complex topic and explains it simply, makes it fun, and gives the reader a practical/useful approach to use in their workplace. Well worth the time it took to read!"

— Gretchen Ann Morris, CISSP, Security Expert

"Jim and Al have created a highly informative, yet entertaining format for all information security practitioners to learn the basics of the IT Security trade. They have clearly presented understanding, selling, motivating, and making information security the basic points in their book. The novel story telling mode of imparting this information works very well."

— Lew Wagner, CPP, CISSP, Chief Information Security Officer, Clarian Health Partners, Inc.

D0067443

KNOW

Cyber Risk

BY MANAGING YOUR IT SECURITY!

James P. Litchko
Al Payne, CISSP

Know Book Publishing
Kensington, MD
www.knowbookpublishing.com

KNOW **Cyber Risk**
By Managing Your IT Security

James P. Litchko
Al Payne, CISSP

Published by:

Know Book Publishing
P.O. Box G
Kensington, MD 20895

info@knowbookpublishing.com
http://www.knowbookpublishing.com

All rights reserved. No part of this book may be reproduced or transmitted in any form or by any means, electronic or mechanical, including photocopying, recording, or by any information storage and retrieval system, without written permission from the author, except for the inclusion of brief quotations in a review.

Printed in the United States of America
First Edition
Copyright ©2004 James P. Litchko

ISBN 0-9748845-1-0

LCCN 2004110406

This publication is sold with the understanding that neither publisher nor author is engaged in rendering advice for specific organizations or IT systems. Expert services should be sought for securing, managing, or promoting specific IT systems and organizations.

Cover and Interior design by: Kristin L. Adolfson
All images ©2004 Kristin L. Adolfson

DEDICATION

KNOW Cyber Risk is dedicated to all the individuals who taught us how to control IT security assessments and how to promote our ideas to management. Thanks to the mentors who provided us with their time, strategies, and encouragement. It was their contributions that allowed us to create this book, so that others can benefit from their knowledge.

FOREWARD

"Have you avoided conducting a security assessment on your systems? Did you not do one because of the fear of not being in control of the process and/or of receiving negative results? Do you see it as an expense without any return-on-investment? If you answered "yes" to any of these questions, you are not alone.

Lack of effective IT security assessments has been a major reason for weak security in both corporate and government IT systems. That is the bad news. The good news is: *KNOW Cyber Risk* now provides IT managers and security professionals with practical strategies and motivational reasons to overcome these fears and concerns.

KNOW Cyber Risk doesn't explain how an IT security assessment is done. There are any number of books that describe assessment techniques. *KNOW Cyber Risk* explains how doing an assessment makes your job easier, how to manage the assessment, and how to use the results to sell security to your boss. To have a successful security program, you need to have the security experts, users, systems managers, and senior management working together. Jim Litchko and Al Payne are security consultants, computer users, IT managers, and corporate executives in commercial and government organizations. They know and understand each player's responsibilities, motivations, and concerns. This awareness has allowed Jim and Al to evolve strategies that help everyone successfully interact with each other and solve IT security problems. The strategies they have presented in *KNOW Cyber Risk* on how to work with security experts, approach security from a business perspective, and sell senior management are right on the mark.

The authors are also educators and business developers, so it is no surprise that their decision to present these strategies in a story format proves to be a highly effective approach on several levels. It helps to provide an informal, relaxed introduction to what most believe is a complicated and stressful subject. Introducing concepts like "Good Security is

B.S.", "Flattery Works", "A rich person is one with options", and "Luck is a loser's crutch" makes the story both entertaining and a quick read – and the concepts easier to understand. Finally, the story format not only helps you understand the strategies, it actually provides a sense of applying them in as a real-world environment.

Having been a security professional for over 20 years myself and read many books on security assessments, *KNOW Cyber Risk* is the first book that tells how to manage assessments and sell the results to management – two critical components to any successful IT security program. If you are looking to make your career more successful and make your job more effective, I highly recommend that you used the strategies presented in this book.

I thank Jim and Al for their work on writing and publishing this book, so the IT community can benefit from their experience, knowledge and skills."

– Dave Cullinane, CPP, CISSP

Dave Cullinane is a highly recognized IT security professional. He is currently the Chief Information Security Officer (CISO) for Washington Mutual, Inc. - one of the largest banks in the United States. Previously, he was the Director of Information Security for Sun Life of Canada's U.S. operations and helped create Digital Equipment Corporation's Security Consulting Practice.

Dave also holds some very important positions in key organizations that are influencing the course of IT security. He is the International President of the Information Systems Security Association (ISSA), the largest international, not-for-profit association for information security professionals. He is the a Charter Member of the Global Council of Chief Security Officers, a group of influential senior cyber-security leaders dedicated to enhancing cyber security. Dave also serves on ASIS International's Information Technology Security Committee (ITSC) and is on the Editorial Advisory Board of CSO Magazine and Security Technology & Design Magazine.

INTRODUCTION

KNOW Cyber Risk is a quick, informal, and entertaining story that provides the reader with answers to the question: "How can I manage a successful IT security assessment?"

Many managers and security specialists in commercial and government organizations have discovered that the four most frustrating duties related to conducting IT security assessments are:

- **understanding** the complex concepts of IT security.

- **selling** the need for security to senior management.

- **motivating** IT managers to request IT security assessments.

- **making** security solutions conform to business needs.

If you are one of these frustrated individuals, this book is a must read, because it was specifically written to reduce or eliminate your frustrations by providing you with successful ways to accomplish these difficult duties.

This story is about Dan, an IT manager, tasked with doing an IT security assessment, working with IT security consultants, and reporting the results to his corporate executives. Sound familiar? Over the course of six weeks, Dan and his three Friday night poker buddies (a cop, a product salesman, and a government bureaucrat) develop the practical strategies that allow Dan to successfully complete his IT security assessment.

The strategies used by Dan are based on the authors' combined 60 years of experience as successful IT managers, security experts, and executives. The strategies address how to successfully:

- **manage** and **control** an IT security assessment.

- **approach** an IT security assessment from a business perspective.

- **communicate** effectively with internal or external security experts.

- **gain** organizational consensus.

- **promote** and **sell** recommendations to executives.

It is the authors' hope that by presenting the development and implementation of these strategies through Dan and his buddies, the readers will gain an applied knowledge of these strategies and use them to be successful in managing their IT security assessments.

– Jim Litchko
  Al Payne, CISSP

Contents

THE
CHALLENGE

THE CHALLENGE

"What could this be about?" Dan thought as he waited for his boss to finish writing a note. He knew of no problems with the large information system that he managed. It couldn't be a personnel review because he had only been on the job for two months. So he wondered, what could this be about?

Finally, his boss put the note in her 'out' basket, looked up from her desk, and said, "Have a seat Dan. I have a critical task that you need to get started on immediately."

Dan sat in the chair closest to her desk. "A critical task? What is it? How can I help?"

"I need you to do a security assessment on your computers and networks," she informed him.

"A security assessment?" he felt as if someone had just kicked him in the stomach.

"Yes, there are several regulations and laws that demand that we have periodic security assessments conducted on all of our computer and network systems. These are to ensure that we are adequately protecting our company resources and shareholders assets. I've checked and none of our IT systems have ever had a security assessment. So, I've decided that your system is the best one to do first, because it's the largest; after yours, the rest will be easy."

"Are you sure? It may be better to start small and build up to a larger system," said Dan too quickly.

"No, I've thought about this all day. I have confidence that you'll do a great job on this," she responded, "Please review what this is going to require, decide on a strategy, and get back to me in a week or so with an implementation schedule."

Well, that was that. Accepting the inevitable, Dan responded, "I will work on it right away."

"Oh, and I have contracted with an IT security consulting firm to support you."

Great, from bad to worse, Dan thought, now I have someone looking over my shoulder who'll report any mistakes to my boss. Dan smiled, "Thank you."

"No, thank you. Relax and have a great weekend."

Dan left her office, feeling like the IRS was about to audit his finances. This is going to be a great, long, miserable weekend, he thought to himself.

Didn't his boss know the management rule that you never give anyone bad news on a Friday?

He kept thinking, "What can I do to get control over this situation?"

Then he remembered some advice his physics teacher in high school had given him. "When you're looking at a new challenge the best thing to do is ask others for ideas and recommendations, and the more diverse they are the better."

Then it came to him. He couldn't get more diverse than his Friday night poker game buddies: Sophie, Paula, and Bill.

Sophie is a successful, government bureaucrat, who views the government as her career Mount Everest to be scaled before retiring. She could help with the organizational challenges, politics, and provide a senior management perspective.

Paula is a street cop; an enforcer of the law. She could make sure that he met all the regulations, identify practical security solutions, and advise him on how to implement them.

Bill is the confident, promoting sales person that would love nothing more than a new challenge to sell anything to anyone.

Of course Dan is the technical, systematic manager. He knew he could count on his IT system know-how and tools to solve the technical problems.

This would be a collaborative effort by all. He could ask them to help him with solving this new challenge, and as luck would have it, tonight was their weekly poker game.

First Game Night

The Dead Man's Hand
The Unknowns

THE DEAD MAN'S HAND

The four sat around Dan's dining room table. The sound of shuffling and dealing cards was punctuated by the stacking and restacking of poker chips. Their weekly poker game had been a ritual ever since they graduated from college.

"What world problems are we going to solve tonight, so we can distract Sophie from winning again?" Bill asked.

"I have the perfect problem, it involves regulations, politics, external experts, risk, security, and my career. Interested?" Dan asked.

All eyes were on Dan. "Risk and security you say?" Paula inquired.

"And a sales challenge, I suspect," added Bill.

"Politics, risks, and careers on the line! Sounds intriguing, let's hear more," said Sophie.

During the next few hands, Dan explained the problem to his friends. When he finished he sat waiting, as if he had just been dealt the 'dead man's hand', the unluckiest hand in poker. The dead man's hand is two pair of black aces and eights, the hand that Wild Bill Hickok held when Jack McCall shot him dead in Deadwood, South Dakota.

After some thought, Paula leaned toward Dan, one hand shielding her cards and the other mid-air to accent her point, "Come on, we do security assessments everyday, why is this any different than driving a car, crossing a road, buying stocks, getting married, having kids, betting on cards, yadda, yadda, yadda? As a police officer, I take risks everyday, but I accept them. I've gotten used to it."

"Yeah, we all do! So why should this particular task have you so gun shy?" Sophie asked.

"Because, this is our first security assessment, and I'm responsible for the IT system being assessed, that's why," Dan tersely responded, a bit frustrated, "I'm afraid the results will reflect badly on my job performance. What if they find something wrong? They'll all be saying, he's the IT guy, so why didn't he know about that problem? Or, did he know about the security problem and hide it? If they find something really bad, can I be held criminally responsible? Will I have to spend my entire budget to fix the problem? Could I lose my job?" Dan sighed.

"Are you sure any of that's going to happen?" Bill asked.

"You don't think someone else is going to take responsibility for security problems, do you?" Dan asked emphatically.

The three looked at each other with questioning stares, trying to think of how to respond, but nothing surfaced.

"Sorry, I didn't mean to be so direct," Dan apologized, "This whole situation has gotten me a little tense."

"Don't worry. Now we understand your concerns," Paula tried to console Dan, "You did say that your boss is getting consultants to help you, right?"

"Sure, but they are usually your typical paranoid security geeks who promote 'FUD', not solutions," responded Dan.

"**FUD?**" asked Paula.

"**Fear, Uncertainty and Doubt**," Bill joined, "It's a professional technique that uses facts and statistics to show everyone in the room that you know more about security than anyone else. It's also used to sell security solutions. You scare the client into buying your solution, by showing them the dire consequences if they don't have it."

"What's the other method?" Paula asked.

"Acronyms! The IT security community is always making up new acronyms to confuse those who attempt to break their technical jargon. This is so they can continue to charge ridiculously high rates for their consulting services."

"They do it all the time to us bureaucrats," Sophie added, "and some government programs use FUD to get their programs funded."

"Really?" Bill responded smirking at Sophie, implying some type of ethical breach in the government.

Before Sophie could respond, Dan continued, "So what should I do? She wants me to report back to her in a week."

"You need a plan," said Sophie.

"Yes, and one that includes the promotion and selling to your executives and users," added Bill.

Paula quickly sat upright and leaned forward, hands on the table, "and proactive interference."

"What are you all talking about?" Dan asked, feeling like the only player in the game that didn't know the rules.

"Dan, what do you do when you play a new card game?" Sophie asked.

"First, learn the rules and the objectives. Second, get to know the players' capabilities, motives, and weaknesses. Then I build a strategy and play my hand." he responded.

"Perfect. It's no different with this task. You need to do the same things for this effort and take charge of the situation," started Sophie.

"Taking charge is the most important thing. You must also play your hand and no one else's," announced Bill.

"Right! You need to manage and control the situation, not avoid it. Also you need proactive interference," concluded Paula.

"**Proactive interference**? What is that?"

"I'm glad you finally asked! It's not letting things just happen and waiting for luck to intervene," Paula responded, "It's taking actions that will ensure success, like briefing your management on the problem, business impacts, and possible solutions days before they need to make a decision."

"Or asking individuals their opinions on your solution prior to calling them all together to make decisions," offered Sophie.

"And publicly giving them credit for their contributions to solving the problem," Bill added.

"Please give me a score pad and let me take some notes," Dan requested of Paula.

SCOREPAD

WHEN CONFRONTED WITH
SOMETHING NEW:

-MANAGE IT, DON'T AVOID IT.

-UNDERSTAND THE UNKNOWNS.

-ESTABLISH A STRATEGY.

-TAKE CHARGE.

THE UNKNOWNS

"OK. Where do I begin?" Dan said, almost talking to himself.

"You're a smart guy," Paula said, "You can handle this."

"In the police force, we get nervous when we don't know who is on the other side of the door or corner, and most important what their motivations are. The risk is high, so we immediately assume the worst," she continued.

As a police officer, I like to work a beat, because that way I know the layout of every house, alley, and store on my beat. I know the peoples' cultures, moods, and motivations. With this information, I can predict what may happen when I take an action. It gives me the edge that allows me to take charge of the situation."

"I'm going to need a lot of luck to win this hand," Dan concluded.

"Luck is a crutch for losers, who are too lazy to research the game and the players to gain a winner's edge," responded Paula.

Dan let this sink in for a moment. "You're right! I've only been on the job for a couple of months. I mean, I barely know where the bathrooms are. I'm going to need more than luck to win this hand."

"Actually, you can use your new status to your advantage," Bill remarked.

"You mean playing the, 'Ah, I'm the new guy. Can I ask you some stupid questions' act?" Dan asked.

"Correct, especially when conducting your research," Sophie interjected, "As far as doing research, it is a must. We do it all the time in government to analyze who wants what, what influences what, and how to prevent failure. Helps us make less mistakes."

"Sounds like a lot of **CYC**."

"CYC?" asked Paula.

"**'Cover Your Career**,' the polite version of CYA," Bill said looking at Paula. Turning back to Dan, he added, "It is CYC, but it is also necessary to move things in your favor. You need to understand the competition's strategy and the desires of the buyer," he added, "In this case, I think the competition is the security consultant and the buyer is your management."

"You make this sound like a war or hostile takeover," Dan stated.

"Well, that analogy has a bit of truth to it. It also provides the right urgency and perspective," Sophie concluded.

"Good! Let's start with the unknowns," Paula began as she leaned toward Dan, "Warning, Dan! This is going to result in you doing a lot of leg work."

Dan grabbed the score pad and pencil, "I'm ready."

They all fired questions at him one after another.

"What is the goal of this security assessment?"

"Why do you have to do a security assessment?"

"Is it driven by regulation, law, or fear?"

"What does a security assessment consist of?"

"Who is responsible for doing what?"

"What are the advantages?"

"What are the disadvantages?"

"Who is involved?"

"Who should be involved?"

"What are the players' motivations? Now, that will be a tough one, but Bill and Sophie can help you with that."

"Where is the organization in their budget cycle?"

"Wait a second," Dan halted the bombardment, "what does the budget cycle have to do with this?"

"We'll answer that later," responded Sophie, "That's enough for now. If you get the answers to most of those questions before next Friday's game, we can help you build a winning strategy," she concluded.

Dan looked around and noticed Paula and Bill nodding in agreement. He looked at the list and quickly realized the magnitude of the task that had just been given to him.

He muttered to himself, "This is going to be a long week."

The others watched as Sophie swept up the last pot with both hands, realizing that the conversation had not broken her concentration enough for her to lose. Dan jotted down some additional notes.

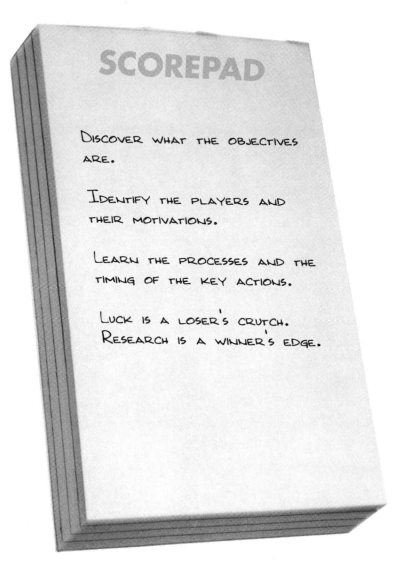

SCOREPAD

Discover what the objectives are.

Identify the players and their motivations.

Learn the processes and the timing of the key actions.

Luck is a loser's crutch.
Research is a winner's edge.

Second Game Night

The Game
The Rules
The Players

THE GAME

The next poker night arrived almost too quickly for Dan. It was a quarter past seven on Friday, and the players were getting comfortable, making sure their drink, snacks, and poker chips were within easy reach.

Part of the evening ritual was to play a practice hand to see who would deal first.

Sophie began dealing the practice hand.

"So, Dan, how was your week?" she asked.

"Very busy, and I only got part of the answers to the questions that you all gave me," he responded, obviously disappointed.

"What did you learn?" Paula said.

"Well, I learned a lot about what security assessments are and why they're necessary."

"OK, let's begin with the 'What?'"

"A security assessment is a cyclical process that reviews an IT system's security to determine what the appropriate level of security should be, what the risks are, and if there is a contingency plan to recover from any security incidents."

"You said it is a cyclical process. What do you mean by that?" asked Bill.

"Good question. Let me show you." Dan said as he drew six ovals in a rough circle on a score pad.

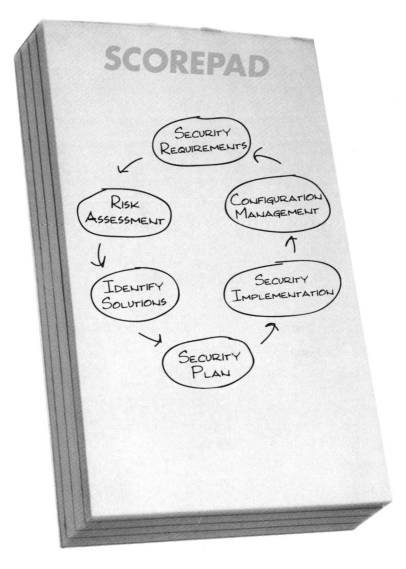

After linking the ovals together in a counter-clock wise flow, Dan started, "What I mean is that there are different phases in a security assessment and you have to repeat the process periodically to ensure that you are secure. That's because new vulnerabilities and threats are identified everyday. Also, if you make changes to the system you have to check their impact on the security."

"What are the phases?" asked Paula.

"Depending on the methodology that you use it can run from six to twelve, so let me tell you the basic six: requirements, risk assessment, solutions, security plan, implementation, and configuration management.

"The **security requirements** phase is where you identify what information is sensitive, what services are critical (or must be available), what information must be very accurate, who and what software applications need access to specific information and when, who and what can change it, and so on.

"The **risk assessment** is an evaluation of the system's threats to vulnerabilities in the system, as well as the impacts if the system's security is compromised. The results allow you to set your priorities.

"The **identify solutions** phase is where you identify the right solutions to counter your biggest security concerns."

"Is that where they match the operational and security requirements, conduct the technical compatibility testing, and assess the return-on-investment reviews?" asked Bill.

"Good, Bill," Dan continued with his explanation, "Using what was learned in the previous two phases and what will be determined to be affordable and acceptable, you can also identify what solutions will be deployed. You also identify the **residual risk**, which is when you cannot afford or provide the countermeasures or safeguards to completely eliminate the risk. With residual risks, you have to accept the risk and identify a recovery plan for when the worst happens or you budget for the near-term unaffordable countermeasures."

"Like wearing a bullet-proof vest is great, but your head, arms, and legs are still vulnerable areas," Paula proposed.

"Exactly!" Dan agreed, "Now, the **IT security plan** is where you document what the security policies, individual's roles and responsibilities, safeguards, countermeasures, and procedures are for the IT system. This is a very detailed document that provides everyone with the key IT security reference document on what the roles, rules, and responsibilities are."

"We have an operational plan for various scenarios," related Paula, "The plans covers: Who is in charge? What laws apply: Local, State, or Federal? What facilities are most important and why? What are the rules of engagement? Who talks to the media? What radio frequencies are for what and who? What has priority over what? Is the IT security plan like that?"

"Yes, it is," Dan continued with his explanation, "The **security implementation** phase is where you train your employees and deploy your security countermeasures and safeguards."

"Do they have to periodically re-test the security solutions to ensure they are correctly maintained? Like how we have to re-qualify at the firing range?" asked Paula.

"Yes. It is recommended that we occasionally test and verify the technical, physical, procedural, and personnel solutions to ensure they all work and work well together."

"And the final phase?" asked Sophie pointing to the last circle.

"That is the **configuration management** phase. It is a process of ensuring that updates are made and establishing the continued review of the system's security as the system grows to meet the organization's needs. All changes to the system are reviewed for their impact on the system's security before the system is updated. That is why this has to be a cyclical process."

"Sounds pretty comprehensive," said Paula.

"And expensive," added Bill.

"It can be, if it isn't managed correctly. That's why management needs to lead the effort to keep it focused and to do what makes sense," stated Sophie.

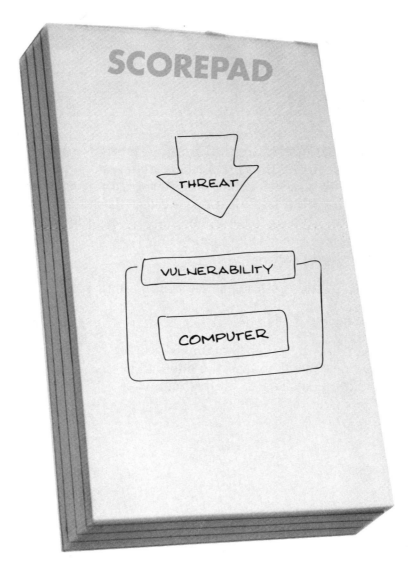

"A main focus is evaluating the risk related to the known threats, IT system's vulnerabilities, and existing countermeasures," Dan explained.

"OK, I know on the street what the threats, vulnerabilities and countermeasures are: robber, window, and big mean dog or me. Bill knows them in his market place, and Sophie knows them in her organization, but how do you define them in an IT system?"

"Good question. The **threats** are things that take advantage of the systems' vulnerabilities, intentionally or unintentionally. Threats include: thieves, hackers, disgruntled employees, three feet, viruses and worms, loss of electrical power, fire, and even leaks in ceilings – computers hate water. Pretty much, threats are insiders, outsiders, natural disasters, and other things."

"Three feet?" asked Sophie.

"Computers don't like heights. At least when they are dropped from heights of 3 feet or higher," clarified Bill, who used to sell computers.

Dan continued, "Thank you Bill. Now, **vulnerabilities** are the weaknesses in the system that someone or something can take advantage of. Examples are: weak passwords, lack of auditing, lack of physical security, no backups, dependency on electrical power, need for dry conditions, software with security holes, and other things like that.

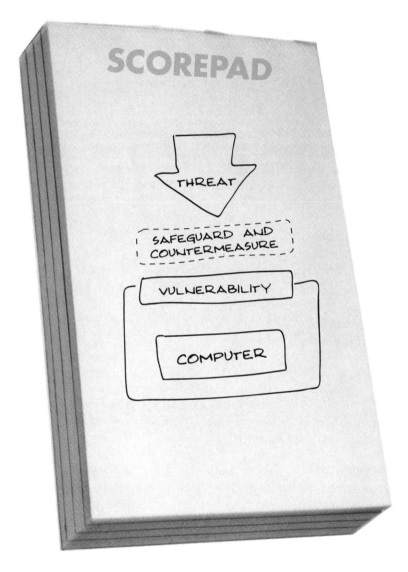

"Finally the **countermeasures** are those things that reduce or eliminate the vulnerability, like a software patch, prevent the threat from exploiting the vulnerability, like a firewall or encryption, or reduce the impact of the attack, like a backup system or recovery plan.

"With all three of these, we can calculate the **risk**, which is how probable it is that a threat will exploit a vulnerability and what will be the impact when that happens."

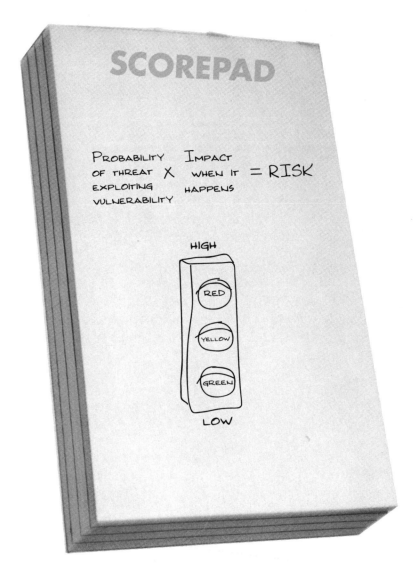

"So is the risk evaluated as high, medium, or low?" asked Sophie.

"High, medium, or low. Red, yellow, or green. It depends on the security consultant's judgment or the risk analysis tool used."

"Or, who you are selling to," responded Bill.

"Interesting and true, because in the end you use the risk to determine what countermeasure is best and to sell to management," Sophie thought out loud, then said, "Give us an example of an IT security risk."

Dan thought for a moment and said, "Here's one. Let's say there is a virus that is programmed to attack a software vulnerability and its mission is to destroy all the system's files. We have three countermeasures we can apply:

- Install **updates**.

- Deploy **anti-virus software**.

- Create frequent **backups**.

"If we install a **patch** or **update** to eliminate a hole in the system, we are still at risk if a new vulnerability is identified.

"If we install **anti-virus** software, we further reduce our risk, leaving us with the potential of being attacked by the new virus before receiving the anti-virus definition for the new virus.

"If we do **backups** frequently, we further reduce the costs related to the recovery of the data."

"Interesting," responded Paula.

"How do they go about identifying the vulnerabilities?" asked Sophie.

"Essentially the IT security experts review the system's design, conduct software code reviews, do penetration tests using **red teams**, and interview employees for security awareness," Dan responded.

"What are red teams?" asked Paula.

"They are a group of technical security experts that use various techniques and hacker tools to break into your system and find the vulnerabilities. Sometimes, you will hear them referred to as **white-hat** or **ethical hackers**."

"Something is missing here. Threats and vulnerabilities are not enough to justify decisions on which security solutions are appropriate," stated Paula.

"Yeah! Where is the identification of the corporate goals and missions, end-user capabilities and expectations, and costs?" asked Bill.

"You're right! During my research, there was never any discussion about the organization, the mission, or the business." Dan said.

"How can they provide recommendations to management, if they don't understand the organization?" asked Sophie.

"I agree." started Bill, "To sell someone a product, I need to understand their problem and what they are willing to accept. Otherwise I'm wasting their time and mine."

"That omission could be something that you can use to your advantage. Make a note of it, Dan, and we'll come back to it later when we're building your strategy," Sophie instructed.

"Is there a standard security assessment methodology?" Paula asked.

"Not really," replied Dan, "it depends on the people conducting the assessment. Some use automated tools, other have their own processes, or follow the DITSCAP or guidance from the NIST. It seems to be more art than science."

"DITSCAP and NIST?" Paula asked.

"**DITSCAP** is the Department of Defense's IT Security Certification and Accreditation Process and **NIST** is the National Institute of Standards and Technology. DITSCAP is the approved process for the agencies and Services in the Department of Defense. NIST provides guidance for commercial and government agencies," he explained, "Management has to decide which is the most appropriate for their organizations."

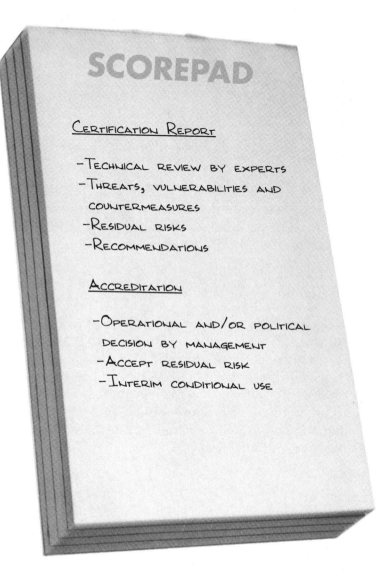

SCOREPAD

<u>Certification Report</u>

- Technical review by experts
- Threats, vulnerabilities and countermeasures
- Residual risks
- Recommendations

<u>Accreditation</u>

- Operational and/or political decision by management
- Accept residual risk
- Interim conditional use

"Basically, the process is that you do a technical security review of the IT system's vulnerabilities, threats, safeguards, and countermeasures. Once this is completed, you identify what is not protected and the residual risk. Finally, you make recommendations on ways to reduce the residual risks. This entire process is called a **system certification**.

"The document that reports all the results of this process to management is called a **Certification or Assessment Report**. This report is reviewed with management, who makes the operational and/or political decisions on what risks they want reduced and which they'll accept. The approval and decisions by management are called the **accreditation**. They can approve the system for operational use, shut it down, or approve it for **interim conditional use** or **interim approval** to operate."

Bill thought for a second. Finally he turned to Dan and asked, "When they conduct a risk assessment is it quantitative or qualitative?"

"Good question. There seems to..."

Paula interrupted, "What do you mean quantitative and qualitative?"

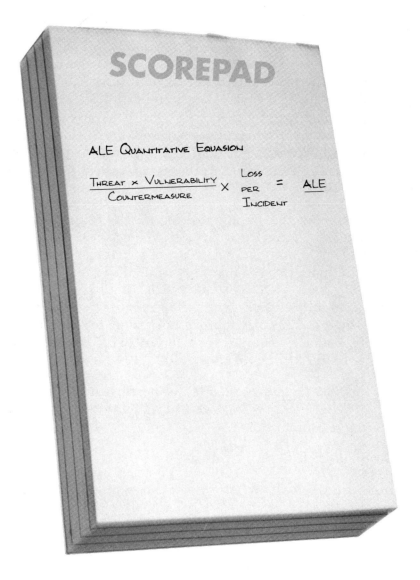

SCOREPAD

ALE Quantitative Equasion

$$\frac{Threat \times Vulnerability}{Countermeasure} \times \frac{Loss}{per\ Incident} = \underline{ALE}$$

"**Quantitative** is when they calculate an **Annual Loss Estimate** or **ALE**, which is the potential loss in dollars per year from attacks by a threat against a vulnerability. The ALE calculation also factors in how effective a countermeasure is in defending against that attack.

"To calculate this ALE, they use various equations. Typically, they are based on the probability of the threat occurring multiplied by a vulnerability value divided by the effectiveness of the countermeasure multiplied by the expected dollar loss per incident. Here let me show you on paper."

Dan took the score pad and wrote out an equation.

"Here we have the basic equation," he began his explanation.

"The **threat value** is the potential times a year that the threat typically attacks a similar system.

"The **vulnerability value** is a '1' if the vulnerability exists in the system and a '0' if it does not exist.

"The **countermeasure value** is a percentage of how effective a countermeasure reduces the impact of an incident.

"The **loss per incident value** is the calculated dollar loss to a company per incident. This could be the cost of replacing information, loss of current and future revenues, fines, lawsuits, impact on image, etc.

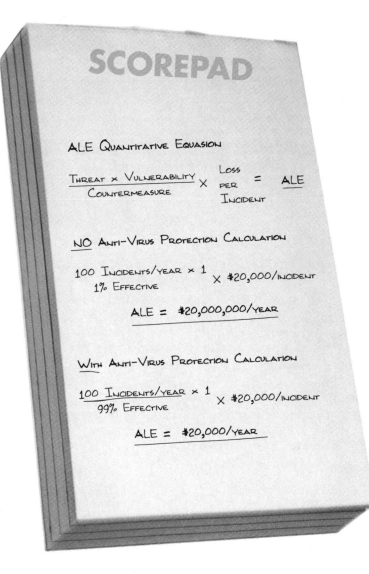

SCOREPAD

ALE Quantitative Equasion

$$\frac{\text{Threat} \times \text{Vulnerability}}{\text{Countermeasure}} \times \frac{\text{Loss}}{\text{per Incident}} = \underline{\text{ALE}}$$

NO Anti-Virus Protection Calculation

$$\frac{100 \text{ Incidents/year} \times 1}{1\% \text{ Effective}} \times \$20,000/\text{incident}$$

$$\underline{\text{ALE} = \$20,000,000/\text{year}}$$

With Anti-Virus Protection Calculation

$$\frac{100 \text{ Incidents/year} \times 1}{99\% \text{ Effective}} \times \$20,000/\text{incident}$$

$$\underline{\text{ALE} = \$20,000/\text{year}}$$

"By sticking these variables into one of a variety of standard equations you calculate the ALE for that type of incident. You then use the result to prioritize the organization's security concerns, conduct cost benefit analysis on potential countermeasures, and justify recommendations."

"Give us an example," Bill requested.

"OK. Let's talk about a virus threat again. Your potential of getting a virus could be about 100 times a year. If you do not have an anti-virus program, you have a major vulnerability. You figure the loss to the company from a virus attack is approximately $20,000 per attack. That figure includes the cost to remove it, restore the data and system, and the loss of revenue, reputation, and potential customers," Dan explained while writing down the results on a score pad, "Total annual estimated loss is $20,000,000 per year."

"Now, if we deploy an anti-virus countermeasure for the cost of $10,000 per year, the end result changes, because we no longer have a 1% effective countermeasure, we have a 99% effective countermeasure," he continued, "that changes the ALE from $20,000,000 to $20,000 a year or about a 2,000% return on your $10,000 investment. The residual risk is $20,000 per year."

"That is a convincing **Return-On-Investment**," Bill responded, "With that **ROI,** I could sell it easily."

"Man, if I did all of that before making a collar, the perp would be out the back door and long gone with the cash," concluded Paula.

"And probably have it spent," added Bill.

"So far it seems that the quantitative method is preferred by accountants, researchers, and consultants that are paid by the hour, and those that learned their security out of a book," said Dan.

"But it could be selectively used to sell managers who make their decisions like those individuals," Bill suggested.

Everyone around the table nodded in agreement and Dan made a note.

"What about the qualitative method?" Paula asked.

"Qualitative risk assessment is similar to Paula and the perp," Dan explained, "Paula mentally reviews several variables: the potential risks to innocent bystanders and herself, how long until backup arrives, and what could happen if the perp gets away. In her mind, she assesses if the risk is high, medium, or low, and then gives herself a red, yellow, or green light to go after the perp. Qualitative assessment on an IT system is the same. It is conducted by someone that is experienced with running IT systems security operations and can determine and justify, if a risk is high, medium, or low for a specific threat."

"The qualitative method sounds more practical to me," concluded Paula.

"For a practical and experienced individual, it is fast and efficient, but a manager must have confidence in the individual who is providing the assessment. He also has to understand the logic well enough to explain it to his management, because it can be pretty subjective," Dan replied.

"Well, from what I've determined, both are very subjective," observed Bill.

"Right, so we can now conclude that there is no one standard process or methodology. That means we have options which provides flexibility. This will allow us to influence and manage the process and/or challenge the results with reasoning that is understood by your management," Sophie said.

"That sounds a bit unethical to me," stated Dan.

"Totally ethical. It's a realistic and practical approach to ensure that the most effective solution is provided," replied Paula, "As my father used to say: 'a rich person is one with options, and a wise person uses them'."

"Good! Now that we've exhausted the 'What', let's move onto the 'Why?'", interjected Bill, "But first, why not increase the risk of you folks losing some money by playing some cards?"

Starting the deal, Paula responded, "I just calculated my risk of losing as low."

"Ante-up and we'll see."

SCOREPAD

CERTIFICATION IS A TECHNICAL EVALUATION OF THE IT SYSTEM'S SECURITY.

ACCREDITATION IS MANAGEMENT'S OPERATIONAL AND POLITICAL DECISION TO ACCEPT THE RESIDUAL RISK.

WHEN THERE ARE MULTIPLE STANDARDS, THERE ARE NO STANDARDS.

FLEXIBILITY PROVIDES OPTIONS. USE IT TO YOUR ADVANTAGE.

THE RULES

Two hours and many hands later, the players took a break to stretch and replenish the snacks. The discussion on Dan's situation continued.

"Why do you have to conduct this security assessment?" asked Paula.

"The government has some regulations and laws that require anyone with an IT system to establish a formal IT security policy. It involves providing employees with IT security awareness training annually, documenting IT system security assessments, and developing a security plan and budget to correct existing security deficiencies," responded Dan.

"Sounds like a good practice. What are some of these regulations? What are the penalties if you don't comply with their directives?" she continued.

"There are several that apply to our organization. **The Gramm-Leach-Bliley Act (GLBA), Federal Information Security Management Act (FISMA), Health Information Portability and Accountability Act (HIPAA),** and **Sarbanes-Oxley (SOX).**"

"This table provides a summary of each of them," Dan provided each with a piece of paper.

"Lots of people use the regulations as a baseline for their policies and justification of their security solutions. Right Sophie?" said Bill.

SCOREPAD

Regulations and Laws

FISMA
Government – OMB
  Annual Cyber Report Card
  and Budget Controls

GLBA
  Financial – FTC
  Audits, Fines, Sanctions, and
  Civil Lawsuits

HIPAA
  Healthcare – HHS
  Stiff Fines and Imprisonment

SOX
  Business – SEC
  Stiff Fines and Imprisonment

"Right, and these regulations provide a good base to start with, because senior managers understand that they can delegate a lot of things to others, but they are still personally accountable for their organization's failure to comply with regulations," she responded.

"I found that each regulation is targeted for a different community, enforced by different government agencies, and has various incentives to motivate management to comply.

"For example, the **Gramm-Leach Bliley Act** requires all financial organizations to take steps to protect the confidentiality of consumer's non-public financial information and it is enforced by the Federal Trade Commission (FTC).

"**FISMA** mandates that the Office of Management and Budget (OMB) ensure that all Federal agencies perform annual security assessments on their IT systems and provide protections commensurate with the risk.

"**HIPAA** requires that all healthcare providers provide adequate protection for patient information in physical and electronic form. The Health and Human Services agency is responsible for enforcing HIPAA.

"**Sarbanes-Oxley** makes it mandatory for CEO's and CFO's to document, test, and fix controls in their systems that certify the accuracy of their financial information. It is enforced by the Securities and Exchange Commission (SEC)."

"Is there any teeth behind any of these?" asked Paula.

"You mean incentives," grinned Sophie.

"No, I mean teeth, like fines, imprisonment, loss of authority, or political embarrassment," she specified.

"For FISMA, the OMB and Congress puts out an annual 'cyber security report' or as the press calls it a 'grade card' for each government agency. OMB also has some control over agency budgets. Under the Gramm-Leach Bliley Act, government agencies can be audited and fined. HIPAA and Sarbanes-Oxley have very specific and impressive fines for non-compliance and they are strongly enforced. The latter can result in up to 15 million dollar fines and 25 years of imprisonment."

"So it looks like the result of the first one is political embarrassment and loss of budget control, and the others have some real teeth," responded Paula.

"Trust me Paula, when someone can take away your ability to control your budget, we bureaucrats see big teeth and pay close attention," corrected Sophie.

"Now let's remember that within all of these are guidelines and mandatory requirements that need to be satisfied using good practical and logical actions," Sophie reminded everyone.

"You mean we don't have to follow the guidelines to the letter?" asked Dan.

"Ha! Doing that would be a government consultant's dream," Bill joked.

"Very true. You want this effort to be supportive, compliant, and effective. Not a career for someone," cautioned Sophie.

"Remember, you must look at the guidelines as just that – not checklists."

"More flexibility, right?"

"That's right. Let me give you an example. Several years ago I was given the task of creating and publishing an organization's budget justification to Congress. That's the document that explained our budget submission to Congress, so they would review, approve, and allocate funds to us in the next fiscal year," started Sophie.

"I had read all the directives on how Congress wanted the justification to look. The directions were very specific on the format, so it was easy to report this to my boss, Betty. 'Betty, we are required to submit the book in the following format: all standard non-glossy 8 1/2 by 11, white paper, landscape, no table of contents, no color, no pictures, no index, stapled in the upper left-hand corner, and one project on a page using title, purpose, budget, justification, and contact format outline. Also, we are not allowed to contact any of the Congressional staffers.'

"My boss leaned forward across her desk, looked me straight in the eye, and informed me, 'You have a good understanding of what the guidelines are. Now here is what our justification is going to look like: glossy, white pages, portrait, table of contents, narrative introduction to the overall program that explains how all the pieces support operational requirements, professional pictures of our operations, a glossary and index, and professionally book bound with a blood-red cover.'

"In total shock, I asked, 'And contacting the Congressional staffers?'

"'One month before the justification is sent to them, we'll invite them to a 'Who We Are' day with donuts and lunch. At that time, we'll provide them with a formal presentation of what we do using the same photos that will be in the book, and introduce them to key members of our staff, who'll be happy to help them in the future. That way when they receive our justification, they'll be familiar with the content and know exactly who to contact when they have any questions.'

"And that's what we did," Sophie finished.

"What were the results?" Dan asked.

"They allocated the funds we requested and Congress held up our book as an example of how to submit a budget justification to Congress," she declared.

"Interesting, but now I have to figure out how to be compliant with these security guidelines."

"In your situation, I recommend that you take the safe route and follow the **prudent man rule**."

Bill jumped in, "What's the prudent man rule?"

"Basically, under the prudent man rule, you exercise both due care and due diligence," Sophie replied.

"Thanks. That helped a lot," he replied.

"Let me finish. **Due care** is when you take the steps that any organization applies to implement security or your industry's best security practices. **Due diligence** is when you use prudent management in the execution of due care."

Sophie quickly continued before Bill had a chance to interrupt with another sarcastic comment, "That means you perform your duties and make decisions in good faith, in the best interest of the company, and with the care and diligence that any ordinary person in a similar position would exercise under similar circumstances."

"So in the end, I have to be knowledgeable; identify several options; make good recommendations; and, justify my affordable, cost-effective, and practical recommendations to management," concluded Dan.

"Looks like you're back at needing to sell to someone," concluded Bill.

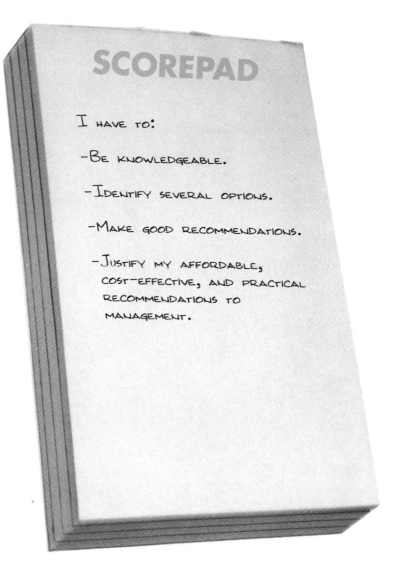

SCOREPAD

I HAVE TO:

−BE KNOWLEDGEABLE.

−IDENTIFY SEVERAL OPTIONS.

−MAKE GOOD RECOMMENDATIONS.

−JUSTIFY MY AFFORDABLE, COST−EFFECTIVE, AND PRACTICAL RECOMMENDATIONS TO MANAGEMENT.

"Correct! Which brings us to the 'Who' of the matter," Paula said.

"First, who wants to play some more cards?" asked Sophie as she shuffled the deck.

"This prudent man does," responded Bill.

"We'll just have to see how prudent that decision is. Ante-up," she said tossing several chips into the center of the table.

SCOREPAD

Understand the rules, best practices, and regulations.

Remember that they are guidelines, not checklists.

Follow the prudent man rule: due care and due diligence.

Do what is practical and logical for your situation.

The Players

After the last hand had been played, everyone helped clean up. When they were finished, Paula said, "Now that was a great poker night. Dan got a lot of advice and we got a lot of his cash."

"Out of respect for that cash and to help Dan with his problem, let's finish our discussion," said Sophie.

"Yes. We need to talk about 'Who' – who'll be involved in the assessment?" asked Bill.

As everyone sat back down at the table, Dan started, "The consultants, management, the users, and me."

"What is each individual's motivation?" Sophie added.

"The **security consultants'** motivation is to demonstrate that they are the experts, to increase the complexity of the effort, to add more of their labor hours to the task, and to justify why their rates are so high," responded Dan.

"Tactlessly direct statement, but from experience, very accurate and realistic," said Bill.

Sophie interjected, "In general that may be true, but let's be cautiously open. I've seen when management's goal is focused the smart consultants provide an efficient, effective, and accurate assessment."

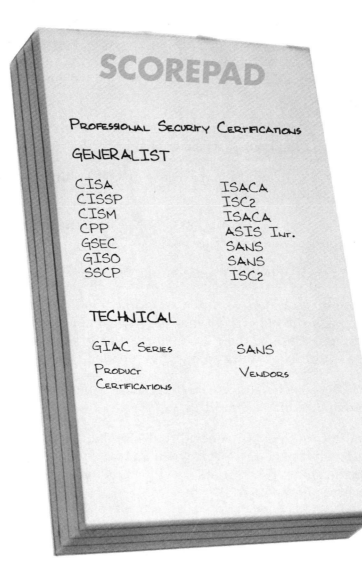

SCOREPAD

Professional Security Certifications

GENERALIST

CISA	ISACA
CISSP	ISC2
CISM	ISACA
CPP	ASIS Int.
GSEC	SANS
GISO	SANS
SSCP	ISC2

TECHNICAL

GIAC Series	SANS
Product Certifications	Vendors

"How do you know if the consultants are qualified?" Paula asks.

"You can tell by the designations after their names, like CISSP, GCIA, GCFW, SSCP, CISA, CPP, CISM, GSEC, and others."

"Sounds like alphabet soup," said Bill.

"The IT security community has multiple professional certifications from the generalist to the technical.

"For the generalist in IT security, the SANS Training Institute has the Security Essentials Certification, with the GSEC designator. The International Information Systems Security Certification Consortium (ISC2), has two: the Certified Information Systems Security Professional and the Systems Security Certified Practitioner, their designators are CISSP and SSCP.

"One that pertains to all security practices is ASIS International's Certified Protection Professional (CPP), and two specific to auditing are Information Systems Audit and Control Association's (ISACA), Certified Information Systems Auditor (CISA), and Certified Information Security Manager (CISM).

"For more technical certifications, the SANS Institute has the Global Information Assurance Certification (GIAC) that provides certifications in technical areas including audit, intrusion detection, firewalls, forensics, and operating system security. Also, there are security product vendors that have their own product certifications."

"Have you validated their certifications with the certifying organization?" asked Sophie.

"Yes, and I also had to ensure that the individuals are certified in the areas for which they are providing their findings and recommendations."

"What about management?" asked Bill.

"I'll answer that," interrupted Sophie, "**Management's motivation** is to understand the risk to their career advancement and protecting their stockholders."

"What else do you have to know about management?"

"I recommend that you do a web search on each so you can see what their backgrounds are," she began, "Knowing how someone thinks and processes information is very important. Managers, researchers, sales personnel, accountants, and engineers process information differently and ask different questions. The better you know your audience the better the chances are you will be able to persuade them."

Bill added, "Also review any presentations, papers or articles that they've presented, written, or been quoted in. Not only do they provide insight to the individual, but they can also provide you with quotes. You can then use the quotes in your presentation to show them that your recommendations are in line with their thinking and goals. Quoting someone is one of the best sources of flattery."

"Makes sense to me," Dan said while making a note on his score pad.

"Let me take the users," offered Paula, "**Users** want to do as little as possible when it comes to security. Whatever we do with the users has to be kept simple. That way when they're interviewed, they provide accurate, but basic, answers."

"A very good assessment," said Dan, "and my motivations are to support operations, have a good grasp on the security of my system, and be able to manage the risks related to the system's day-to-day operations."

"These are good motivations, but be honest, you really don't want to be embarrassed, right?" asked Paula.

"OK, OK. Maybe that's true," he confessed, "but what I said before is also true."

"Hold on a second," Bill began, "I understand the Certification and Accreditation process, but who accredits the system at the end of the assessment?"

"That would be my boss, the Chief Information Officer." Dan said.

"Who does she have to please?"

"Her boss of course."

"And who does she have to satisfy? How are they rewarded? What goals do they need to meet?"

"I get the picture. Obviously, I have some more work to do."

"Yes, but I think the first thing that you need to do is understand the organization's mission or business in terms that management understands."

"Good idea," Sophie said, "That will provide you with a strong justification that the consultants won't be able to respond to. They'll understand the technology, but not the operational reality of the situation."

"That puts you in charge," Bill added.

"You're right, it does," Dan responded as he completed his notes on his score sheet.

"I suggest that we all call it a night, so Dan can get some rest and get an early start on this in the morning," said Paula.

After they all left, Dan reviewed his notes.

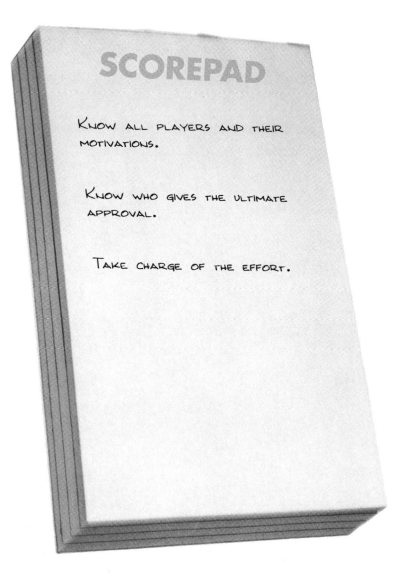

SCOREPAD

Know all players and their motivations.

Know who gives the ultimate approval.

Take charge of the effort.

Third Game Night

The Winning Hand
The Deal
The Pot

THE WINNING HAND

A week later, Dan felt prepared for the poker game. Drinks had been poured, everyone was comfortable, and the second hand of the night was dealt. Dan was ready to discuss what he had learned.

"So Dan, I know you have a lot of new answers for us, but let me ask you a basic question. If we looked at your security assessment problem like a poker game, what would the winning hand look like?" Paula asked as she placed her bet.

"That's a good question, especially when I'm looking at a winning hand," Bill responded as he doubled the bet.

"You're bluffing and you know it," Sophie challenged as she matched the bet.

"Well, I don't need a Royal Flush to win all the time in poker. Similarly, obtaining 100% security is not a practical goal."

"So the **90-10 rule** applies here just like in most projects," Bill said.

Paula looked confused. "The 90-10 rule?"

"In any effort, to get 90% of what you want takes 'X' amount of resources. Then to get the last 10%, it costs you 9 times 'X' in resources," Bill informed the group.

"Basically, Paula, achieving a 100% risk-free system is unaffordable," Sophie said.

Bill smiled. "Exactly."

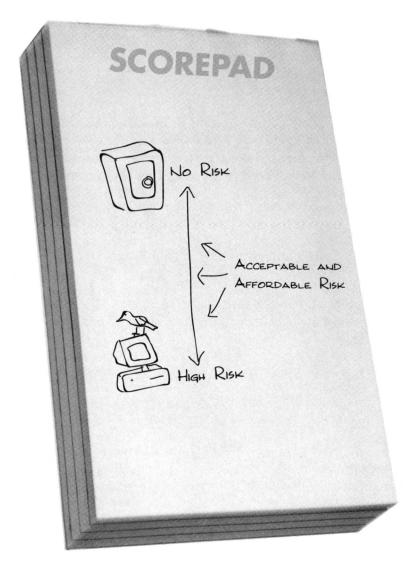

Dan continued, "During my review, I asked the security person what computer security management was about. His response was, 'the secure brick theory'."

"Secure brick theory? I've never heard of that one," said Paula.

"I hadn't either, so he explained it to me:

"The **secure brick theory** is that if you're building a secure computer to fight a war, there are two extremes:

"One is a totally unsecured computer laying in the middle of the battlefield with no protection or cover. Completely open to the weather and anyone that marches by.

"The other is a computer that is so secure that all it is good for is to pick it up like a brick and throw it at the enemy.

"Our job as managers is to determine what the most practical, affordable, and appropriate security level is between these two extremes."

"So, what you need is to draw a poker hand that is a betting hand with an acceptable risk", Paula responded.

Bill piped in, "What does an acceptable risk look like?"

"Something like two pair or three-of-a-kind would be a nice betting hand right now," responded Dan.

"Well, who determines what an acceptable risk is for a specific system?" Bill asked.

"That's a good question. According to the regulations, it's what the accreditation authority will accept."

"Who's the accreditation authority in your case?" Bill continued.

"It shouldn't be Dan," Paula said, "it should be the person who decides that the hand is worth holding, folding, betting, and asks for more cards."

"Yes, it should be the one that makes the operational, financial, and political decisions and has the responsibility under the regulations," Sophie added.

"Exactly! I've learned from the school of hard knocks that you never take on a responsibility without the authority and resources to be successful," Paula replied.

"So, are we talking about the CIO or the head of the organization?" asked Bill.

"Before I answer that, let me give you an example that provides a different perspective. In my research," Dan explained, "I discovered a government organization where the Director decided that he would be the accrediting authority. His decision was based on the fact that the IT system held very sensitive information from commercial companies and the early release of the information would have a major impact on their stock prices. You see, the Director had higher personal political goals, and any public embarrassment resulting from insecurities in the system would have a direct impact on his political future."

"The story goes," he continued, "that when the CIO asked the Director's permission to put the system online, the Director asked, 'How is the security?' The CIO's response was that the contractor had taken care of it. Since the contractor delivered the system at over twice the cost and time originally contracted for, the Director demanded a third-party review of the security."

"What happened?" asked Bill.

"An independent group of IT security experts conducted a quick security assessment on the system. A month later they provided the Director with a list of twenty security deficiencies, including business impacts, recommendations, and options to correcting each of them.

"After reviewing the list with respect to risks and costs, he announced, 'implement the top ten recommendations and put the system online.' He determined that the leftover ten residual risks were acceptable."

"Proving once again that certification is a technical review of a systems' security, and accreditation is an operational, political, and financial decision," Bill responded.

"Yes," Sophie agreed, "So who is the accreditation authority in your organization, Dan?"

"I'll have to have one of the seniors determine that. It's either the CIO or her boss. What I have to do is figure out how to get one of them to accept the responsibility."

"That will have to be a part of your strategy," Sophie stated.

"That's what I need, a good strategy," Dan concluded as he finished writing the key points of the discussion on his score pad.

"Whatever you do, don't use the bluffing strategy that Bill just used, because he just lost the pot," concluded Sophie as she pulled in her winnings, "Thank you for your donations."

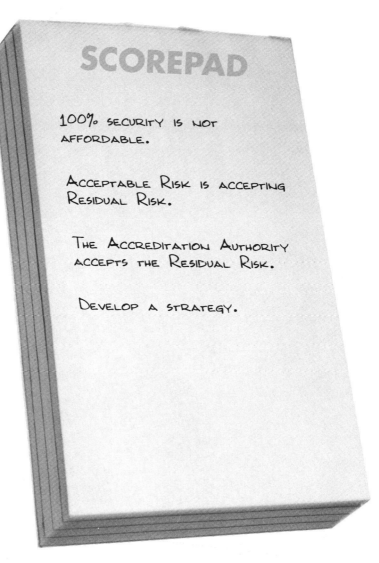

SCOREPAD

100% SECURITY IS NOT
AFFORDABLE.

ACCEPTABLE RISK IS ACCEPTING
RESIDUAL RISK.

THE ACCREDITATION AUTHORITY
ACCEPTS THE RESIDUAL RISK.

DEVELOP A STRATEGY.

THE DEAL

"Before we move to developing a strategy, tell us what hand you've been dealt? What does your IT system look like?" Sophie asked, "What are the security requirements for the current system?"

"We have to keep the individual client's information secure and accurate, so we have confidentiality and integrity requirements," Dan replied, "The clients are authorized to see their information on demand, but in order to maintain privacy, they need to identify and authenticate themselves before they can view their information."

"What do you mean by authenticate?" Paula asked.

"**Authentication** is when users prove to the system that they are who the say they are, so the system can provide them access to the data and programs that they are authorized to work with. They have to provide something that is only known by the system and the individual, like a password, personal identification number, or they use some type of technical authentication device like a smartcard, challenge-response calculator, token, fingerprint reader, or iris scanners."

"Is that like non-repudiation?" Sophie asked.

"**Non-repudiation** is similar. Authentication is like having a combination to a safe or the key to your house. It allows you access to things. Non-repudiation is like having a signature on a check or contract. For that you need strong authentication, because with non-repudiation someone can take it to the courts if they need to.

"Additionally, we need to make the information available to them at all times. So our system needs the typical **CIA** security functions: **Confidentiality**, **Integrity**, and

Availability. Confidentiality is when you only allow authorized people to see sensitive information. Integrity is ensuring that the information is accurate. Availability is having the information and computer processing capabilities when they are needed by the users.

"Finally, in order to be compliant with the various laws and regulations, we need to have **auditing** capabilities."

"That's a lot! Are all of these security requirements needed for the entire system?" Paula asked.

"It's one system, so of course it does. Why?"

"Well, on the police force, we're often asked by people about improving their home and store security. When we make recommendations, we ask questions like:

What are the most valuable items?

Who really needs to get to them, why, where, and when?

Why do they need to get to them and how often?

"Things like that," Paula closed.

"Why do you have to ask those questions?" Dan asked.

"Because we know from experience that all system components need the same level of protection and everyone doesn't need the same access to all the information and programs," answered Paula, "The answers to those questions allow us to recommend the appropriate security that allows individuals to have access to only those items they are authorized to have. With this approach, we save the owners lots of time and money."

"How do you identify what security they need?"

"First we never talk about security, we talk about their business and how they live."

"Not security?"

"If you start talking about security, they get nervous; talk about their business and family and they get relaxed and chatty. Let me give you an example. The other day, I was helping a neighbor to secure his house. By the time we finished talking about his personal life and business, I had identified where they kept valuables, medications, financial papers, etc. Also, who was allowed to have access to what in the house."

"Interesting," said Dan, "but how does that…"

"Let me finish my example. The way they ran their daily lives was on a family business model. Each item in the house required different access controls and individuals had different types and frequency of access to them. Just because they have a gun or a gold bar doesn't mean you change the house into a fortress.

"So my recommendations were to put deadbolt locks on all the external doors. Have all of the locks keyed the same, except for one. I recommended that one have a different key and have a floor bolt. That door is for the maid and over-night guests. The floor bolt is bolted all the time, except on Wednesday when the maid comes and when guests are out. This also provides an added advantage when you fire the maid or a guest loses a key, you only have to change one lock.

"Keep the basic doorknob button locks for the bedrooms and bathrooms, with the parents holding the override key.

"Install a small security safe in a locking closet in the parent's bedroom. This safe is for jewelry, guns, or gold bullion, and the closet locks to protect heirlooms. Parents are the only ones with the keys.

"Buy a filing cabinet that locks to store financial papers.

"Rent a safety deposit box at the local bank to store original ownership and insurance papers, with additional copies in the filing cabinet at home for quick access.

"Fit the cleaning closets with child-proof locks.

"You see, by identifying the specific requirements, I replaced turning the house into a fortress with a total security solution that is practical, user-friendly, and affordable."

Dan thought for a moment. "Now you have me thinking about who really needs access to what in the system. You're right. Everyone doesn't need the same level of access to the different types of information."

Sophie added, "I recommend two things. First, when you pull a group of employees together to identify the business requirements for the system, include the users, administrators, security and operations personnel, and managers.

"By having the various individuals there, you'll get several things: more practical ideas, collaboration, ownership, and awareness.

"By working the problem together, the group will gain an awareness of the systems' processes, capabilities, priorities, sensitivities, and business and security requirements. This overall awareness will allow them to contribute and feel a part of the development of the solutions. Through this collaboration they will gain ownership over the final recommendations. With this ownership, the group will support your requests for additional resources and will be your on-site advocates when the solutions are being implemented," she concluded.

Dan agreed, "That sounds perfect."

"Second, talk to them about how the system works to support the business operations, not about the security," Sophie continued, "If you start talking to the group about security, you'll get the same unsupportive response that a taxpayer would give if an IRS auditor offered to help balance their checkbook.. Taking this business approach, you'll find that they'll be more cooperative and supportive."

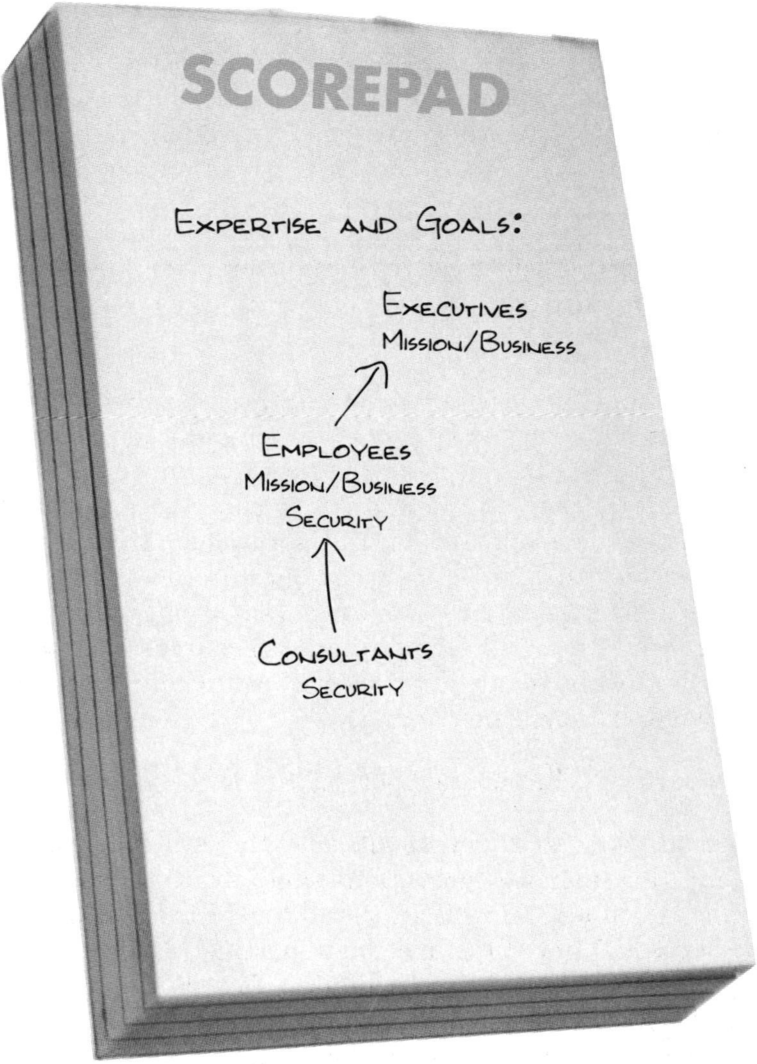

SCOREPAD

Expertise and Goals:

Executives
Mission/Business

↗

Employees
Mission/Business
Security

↑

Consultants
Security

"Whoa, you may have just stumbled on to two more important keys that will help you successfully manage this effort," announced Bill.

"Is this going to be some kind of ethical approach or a sales ploy?" Paula asked with justified suspicion.

"Both. First, by using this approach, you'll be provided with an opportunity to observe each of the players and gain an understanding of what makes each of them tick. You'll also come to know what their real motivations are and how they process information. Once you figure out what their needs are you can show them how this solution fits their needs."

"What is the second key?" Paula asked.

"Approaching this based on business requirements allows you to justify your solutions to senior management in a way that the security experts cannot."

"By driving the security assessment from a mission or business perspective, you control the assessment," Paula said.

"And that is the only perspective your senior management needs to understand," added Sophie.

"Also, use what you use when you are making decisions in cards: your good judgment. With those three keys, I think that you'll be a winner," Paula added.

Finishing his notes, Dan smiled, "I like it."

"Good, because you're not going to like this," Bill said as he turned over his hole card showing three-of-a-kind, beating Dan's two-pair.

SCOREPAD

IT Security is based on business needs first.

Involve the majority of the players to gain their awareness and ownership.

Sell management on security using business logic.

THE POT

As Paula finished shuffling the cards and began to deal, Sophie asked, "Speaking of business, did you learn anything about the budget process?"

"No. None of my peers seems to know or care," stated Dan.

"That's typical, but you need to follow the **Golden Rule: He who has the gold, makes the rules**," said Bill.

"As painful as it is to admit, Bill is right. My recommendation is that you go directly to the people that create the budget," offered Sophie.

"Are you kidding? They are the most demanding, last minute, detailed-oriented, and unfriendly people on the face of the earth," announced Dan.

"Many people have that opinion of them," said Sophie, "but in my experience those opinions come from their lack of understanding the budget process. The only interface they normally have with budgeters is last minute budget memos demanding inputs ASAP.

"So, you need to meet on their terms. Go to their offices and ask them about their goals, processes, and schedules."

Bill was about to speak, but Paula cut him off, "I know what you are going to say Bill, 'and flattery works'."

"That is very true. Personally, I have found that budgeters can be cooperative, flexible, and highly receptive to good justifications," Bill finished. "The fact that everyone treats them as if they were lepers makes them potential business partners for anyone that wants to help them get their job done. That gives you the motivation and a money connection."

"Again, Bill is uncharacteristically correct," Sophie announced with a veiled look of amazement at Bill and then continued on with her explanation, "Whenever I was put into a new position, the budgeters were the first group that I approached. Normally, I would introduce myself as the lost, new person, wanting to understand the budget process so I could be more responsive to their requests. In that way, I was able to influence a lot of funding, in and out of the cycle, and solve lots of problems. That got me the reputation of being a problem solver and led to all my challenging jobs and career promotions."

"I'm all for that," Dan replied.

"Good, and I'm for playing cards, so let's focus our attention on the cards for the rest of the night." Paula said, "I'm high with a pair of aces. I bet two, hold, or fold ladies."

SCOREPAD

Know the "Golden Rule":
  "He who has the Gold, makes
  the Rules."

Know how to influence the
gold.

Know the people, goals,
processes, and timing.

Use your judgement.

Flattery works.

Fourth Game Night

The Bluff
The Odds
The Cool Deck

THE BLUFF

The next scheduled poker night began with much anticipation of how Dan's project was proceeding, since all the players now had a vested interest in his challenge.

Placing the snacks on the table, Sophie eagerly asked, "How's the security assessment going?"

"Great!"

"Do you mean that, or is that something Bill taught you to say to impress others?" asked Paula while she dealt the first hand.

"Both!"

"You sure sound sincere and confident, so it can't be all Bill's questionable influence," she replied, "What have you learned so far from the security assessment?"

"Mainly that the business approach is working great. Just from what I learned this week about the individual user's expectations is going to make my management of the IT system much more efficient."

"Really?"

"Really! Just knowing that our Internet clients will accept day long outages, except on the last two days of the month, and that my management requires minimal outages on the links between the headquarters and the branch offices only during our work hours, allows me to determine how fast I have to respond to outages. That's going to save me lots of resources and cause fewer disruptions during my poker nights."

"Fantastic! What else have you learned?"

"Well, that Bill's **picture**, **reference**, and **wait-time techniques** really work. They have made my relationship with the security experts much more effective and their outputs more useful."

"What's he talking about? I hope these are not some of those slippery sale's cons of yours," Paula asked Bill.

Looking up slowly from his cards, Bill said, "What, me? Never! These methods are simple but highly honored, effective sales and teaching concepts. Used correctly they increase your chances of closing a deal and getting people to understand complex stuff."

Sophie and Paula looked at Bill suspiciously, as they waited for an explanation from the infamous 'Bill the Bluffer'. Bill laid his cards down and started to explain, "First, I will explain the **picture technique**. In my experience, 95% of the people in the world are visual learners. They understand explanations faster if you draw them a picture. So I recommended to Dan that whenever the security experts begin talking in their confusing 'lingua securita', that he stop them and ask them to draw him a picture of what they are talking about."

"Ah, a picture is worth a thousand words."

"Right, and it works!" Dan exclaimed, "I also learned two other things: how to say 'Can you please say that in a different way?' and how to compliment them on their ability to teach me new things."

"Once again, flattery works," Bill added.

"Right! Those two things truly changed our way of working together. Our relationship is much better, because they see me as being interested in learning and accepting them as experts."

"And the **wait-time** and **reference techniques**?" Paula asked.

"During our discussions, I was getting frustrated with the experts constantly saying the IT system was vulnerable to 'this and that', 'these and those', etc. I felt like I was receiving the old FUD treatment, so I called Bill."

"In sales," Bill began, "we refer to statistics to help the customer justify and qualify the value of buying our solutions. I also learned that when you give the customer the price and ask if they want to buy, you should shut up and wait for their response, no matter how long it takes for them to respond. I once had a large deal with a couple where I had to wait 19 minutes for their response, but it was worth it. I waited and closed the deal."

"Interesting. We use the same wait-time technique during criminal interrogations. We ask a question and wait for a response. People seem to have a craving to fill verbal voids and typically end up spilling their guts," Paula added.

"Sales people probably learned it from the police," offered Bill.

Paula was not sure if she should take that as criticism or a compliment, so she just looked at Bill with suspicion.

"How did you use this technique, Dan?" Sophie asked.

"In order to get more clarification so I could set my priorities and develop my justifications, I asked the security experts to provide me with actual references on the risk potential and statistics that they were quoting. Many times they would look at me as if no one ever asked them to do that before. That's when I used wait-time. After waiting ten to twenty seconds, they typically said that they will have to get back to me. I also made sure that they saw me take notes, so they knew that I would not forget.

"After two days of asking for the specific references and waiting, they now provide me with the references without asking. They are also careful about providing me with only the meaningful threats and vulnerabilities."

"Make sure you keep those pictures and references," Sophie said, "I'm sure they'll come in handy in the next two weeks."

"Trust me, I am. Just like I'm always taking notes on our poker games."

"Well, take note of this – a full house," Bill announced as he laid out the winning hand.

SCOREPAD

Understanding the real system's needs helps set real priorities.

Pictures really are worth a thousand words.

Ask for specific references to verify facts.

Wait as long as it takes to get an answer.

The Odds

Collecting the cards, Paula asked, "What issues have been identified so far?"

"So far we have been able to correct many of the issues with procedural, personnel, physical and reconfiguration solutions. By the way Paula, thanks for talking to my group about the total security approach. It was very helpful in putting all of the participants into a more open frame of mind to both technical and non-technical solutions."

"I thought it would help. That approach has always provided me with a more practical and holistic view of securing things," Paula responded, while shuffling the deck.

"Total security? Sophie asked.

"Holistic?" asked Bill.

"**Total security** and **holistic** refers to looking at the entire environment and all potential security solutions. You see, sometimes physical, personnel, and procedural security solutions are better than the technical solutions."

"Total security also comes with the rule that **you can provide total security solutions, but you can never make something totally secure**," Paula added.

"Residual risk," concluded Bill.

"Correct."

SCOREPAD

Total Security Approach and Holistic View:

- Looking at the entire environment and

- All potential security solutions.

Sometimes physical, personnel, and procedural security solutions are better than the technical solutions.

A system can have total security, but it can never be totally secure.

"Again, what security issues have you discovered in your system?" Paula moved the discussion forward as she began dealing the cards.

"The lingering issues are related to low user awareness, limited recovery planning, lack of configuration management, and weak passwords."

"Sounds like you're focusing in on the real problems and recommendations," said Bill.

"I have something that may help," began Sophie, "During the time I was selling our organization's budget, I learned that when you are asking someone to approve something, you should convince them that it meets their goals, not your goals."

"Right," Bill agreed, "and I think our business-based approach supports meeting your managements' goals."

"Agreed," Dan said.

Sophie added, "Another thing I learned was that when you develop a recommendation for someone, you provide them with options. By providing options, you are allowing the client to make a 'one, two, or three' decision instead of a 'yes' or 'no' decision. Providing a client multiple options increases your probability of getting a positive decision. I find this approach most effective when you are not sure how much funding is available."

"That's the same approach we use in sales. It provides a better chance of closing a deal. We all know from the streets that a rich person is one with options," Bill injected, "Right, Paula?"

Paula nodded in agreement, "Also, it will show you respect your senior manager's ability to make good judgments."

"So are your issues conducive to providing multiple options?" asked Sophie.

"You know, I think they are," Dan said, "For awareness, I could propose giving lectures, interactive computer programs, buttons, and posters.

For authentication, the options are using cracker checks for weak passwords and authentication tokens.

"For configuration management, I could recommend automated updates, a central management board that reviews and approves all system changes, and testing software by a third-party expert."

"Sounds like you are not betting on closing an inside straight," Sophie concluded, "Now you just need to decide what the odds are, what the right bet is, and when to place your bet."

"Tricky, but I feel confident that I can do it," he responded, as he looked up from his notes.

"Hey! I have some options for you, Dan," Paula announced, "Match the bid, raise the bid, or fold your cards. I just bid five on my winning hand."

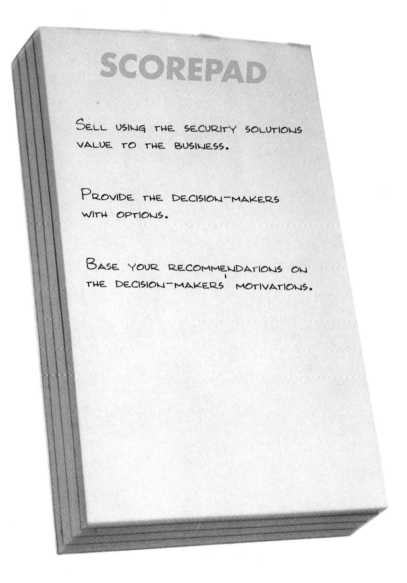

SCOREPAD

Sell using the security solutions value to the business.

Provide the decision-makers with options.

Base your recommendations on the decision-makers' motivations.

The Cold Deck

The poker night was over and everyone was getting ready to leave. Dan said, "Well, I've got my action items for next week."

"You have one more, you should pre-brief your senior management," Sophie said as she put on her coat.

"But I was planning on presenting the results to them at the end!"

"In management, we have a rule: **No one likes surprises**. The one group that you do not want to surprise is your senior management, especially when you'll need their support."

"That's true. Buyers and decision makers do not like to be rushed into something. You want to convince them slowly," provided Bill.

"So, what do I tell them?" Dan asked.

"You only want to tell them that you'll be providing them with the final report and an executive overview presentation. And that during the presentation you'll outline the risks, solution options, and costs," responded Sophie.

"Also, you'll need to make them aware that they will have to decide what level of risk they will be willing to accept," Paula injected.

"And that they will need to decide at the meeting or shortly thereafter," Bill added.

"The whole presentation should take about five to seven minutes and four to five slides. They'll probably want to ask some questions," Sophie added.

"Five minutes!" Dan exclaimed, "How can I explain what the security assessment, certification, and accreditation process is in five minutes!"

"These are senior managers who make decisions. They do not want to personally know how to conduct a security assessment. They only want to know what is coming and that they'll need to make decisions that will have business, operational, political, and financial risks," Sophie explained, "Trust me, if they want more specifics they'll ask."

"They'll also provide you with guidance, so take good notes. Their guidance will be very useful in selling them your solutions at the final meeting," Bill added.

"So the presentation is a heads-up for them and a research gathering exercise for me."

"Exactly," Sophie concurred, "and you should do this alone, not with the security experts, who'll probably request that they do the presentation or attend. If they offer, thank them for the offer and tell them that it's an internal update for the executives and they'll not be needed. Your goal is to give your seniors confidence that you're in charge of this effort."

"I understand" Dan responded as he looked up from his notes.

"See you next week and good luck."

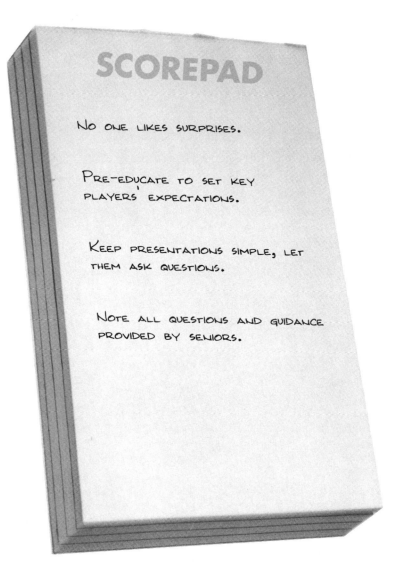

SCOREPAD

No one likes surprises.

Pre-educate to set key players' expectations.

Keep presentations simple, let them ask questions.

Note all questions and guidance provided by seniors.

FIFTH GAME NIGHT

THE BANK
THE PLAY

THE BANK

The next Friday night was different than the rest. The weather had gone bad, strong winds and falling trees had brought down power lines and all of their houses were without electricity. Paula, Sophie, and Bill insisted on holding the game as usual and brought in the back-up resources: kerosene lamps, bags of ice, and an ice chest. It was unclear just why they did not agree when Dan suggested canceling it, but he had a feeling that they wanted to support him during the final and most critical phase of his strategy.

After the kerosene lamps were lit, the players settled down in their chairs, and the discussions began.

"So Dan, how was last week?" asked Paula, as she shuffled the cards.

"Great!" Dan was enthusiastic, "We completed the assessment. More importantly, I know where the money is, who determines where it goes, and when they decide."

"That's great. How did you get that information?" Sophie asked as she restacked and repositioned her chips.

"Just as you suggested, I went to the budget and accounting folks. You were correct, they are very nice people and were very helpful after I showed a sincere interest in learning what they were doing."

"What did they tell you?" asked Bill.

"There are two processes; building next year's budget and spending this year's funds. Some organizations spend one to three years planning and programming for what the future year's budgets will be."

"In the government it's usually a two year process, the final year is when headquarters reviews and allocates the budget to the departments. Pretty much after that you can move the funding around for projects if you have good justifications," Sophie explained.

"Our organization does it in one year. Currently, we are in the approval phase of the budget process for next year. So I'm not late in influencing where the funds are spent next year. The other good news is that we are in the last quarter of this fiscal year. The better news is that other departments have not spent all of their money, so with good justification in my funding request, I can influence some of this year's money."

"What kind of documentation are they asking for to request additional funds?" asked Bill.

"One page! That's all. I just need to ensure that it includes a strong, short, mission-based paragraph justifying the requirement, not a twenty-page technical paper. I can use the certification report and the specific references from the consultants to strengthen the justification.

"And Sophie, you were correct. They like to see funding options in the requests, because it allows them more flexibility in allocating funding that they have."

"That's very good. Now who makes the decisions on these requests?" asked Bill.

"That's the better news. The decision makers are all the people that I'll be briefing next week: the CFO, Director of Personnel, COO, and CIO. The only other person in the funding decision process that will not be in the meeting is the organization's Director."

"Is there any chance of getting him at the presentation?"

"You mean getting *her* there. My plan is to pre-brief my boss on Monday for her suggestions on how I can improve the presentation. If she likes the presentation, she will invite the Director, because it'll make her look good."

"Treating the boss as a mentor and advisor is always a very good approach," said Paula.

"As you all have taught me, flattery works."

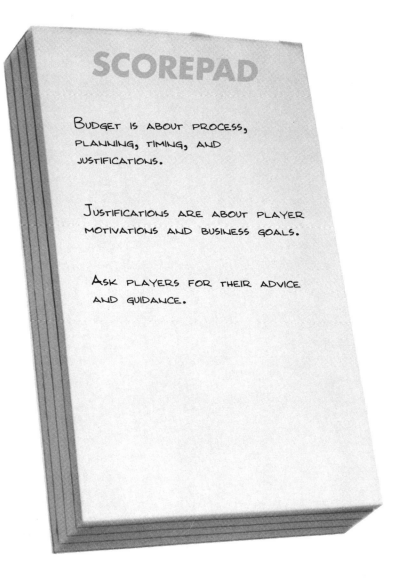

SCOREPAD

Budget is about process, planning, timing, and justifications.

Justifications are about player motivations and business goals.

Ask players for their advice and guidance.

THE PLAY

An hour later, after refilling the glasses, snack bowls, and kerosene lamps, they returned to the game.

"So Dan, this Thursday is the showdown for the security assessment. You and your senior management will place the final bets and show all of your cards," Bill said.

"Yeah, Thursday I'll 'call' them and they'll have to show their hands or fold."

"The fact that you pre-briefed them will make your presentation go a lot easier for you and them," Sophie added.

"How much time will you have to brief them?" asked Bill.

"I figure 15 minutes and 15 more for discussion."

"I recommend that you do the presentation in 10 minutes and quickly get to the decision points. That will show them that you respect their time," Sophie said.

"The consultants said that the management really needs to understand what was done during the assessment, so they can appreciate the work that went into this effort."

"What they really mean is so the management can appreciate the effort that the consultants put into the effort. This is *your* show. Your bosses will only want to hear about the results and what decisions they have to make. Security is not the only thing the senior managers are responsible for," responded Sophie.

"I agree. Also, no one can sell your solutions better than you," Bill added.

"Both of you are right. That is why I'm presenting the information to the seniors."

"Good," his three buddies all agreed.

"OK, so here's my idea on the final presentation. I do the presentation with the key members of the task group in attendance. One slide on what we did. At this point, I'll give credit to the members of the task group, their bosses, and the contractors, for helping to improve our IT system security."

"Aren't you going to say that you coordinated and managed the entire effort?" Paula asked.

"I've learned that by giving credit to others, they'll support me more on future efforts."

"I know, I know, flattery works," Paula admitted.

"Besides, knowledgeable seniors know who was responsible for pulling this effort together. You're better off giving the credit and not asking for it," noted Sophie.

"Right! The next slide will cover what we found and fixed. Then the next three slides will cover each of the three residual issues. Each slide will identify the issue, potential business impacts, options, costs, and recommendation.

"In the last slide, I'll provide my recommendations and how they relate to this year's and next year's budgets."

"That sounds very good," Sophie said, "Can you give us an example of an issue and your recommendations?"

"Awareness is a good one. Our user awareness is poor at best, and is one of the main vulnerabilities of our IT system. Some say the majority of all IT security losses are the results of insider actions. We need to move our users from being vulnerabilities to being countermeasures.

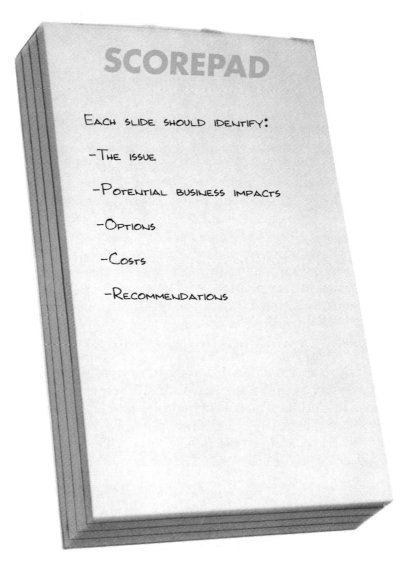

SCOREPAD

Each slide should identify:

- The issue

- Potential business impacts

- Options

- Costs

- Recommendations

"A good awareness program can do that by teaching them how to recognize a potential virus infection and who to call when they suspect one, how to approach an unknown visitor, and who to report suspicious activities to.

"Here we have three options. The first and least expensive are security posters and computer screen security reminders. That cost is about $5,000 per year. These are more effective as periodic reminders of the need to be secure.

"The second option is to provide annual group security lectures for all employees. This cost can range from $5,000 to $30,000 per year, depending on how much outside help we get to support the presentations. There is a hidden cost which is the coordination and administration of pulling all the people and presentations together. Also, there is the cost of monitoring who went and who did not. This is necessary because the regulations require an annual report of who in an organization received security awareness training. With the size of this organization, I would expect that we would need one or two additional people to manage and coordinate this option.

"The third option is an interactive course of instruction that the users can take at their desktop computer whenever they have the time. The software program runs on a system server, automatically monitors the progress of each employee, and compiles reports on demand. The cost is about $30,000 for the license and $10,000 to tailor it for our organization.

"My recommendation is that we procure the posters out of this year's budget and make a down payment on the interactive course to get the basic course tailored to our mission and culture. Next year, we license the software for the interactive course. At the beginning of next year we provide the employees with the interactive course and reinforce need for security with the posters. The cost will be $15,000 for this year and $30,000 for next year."

"Aren't you going to compare this with what an employee costs for a year so they can see what the additional overhead cost of option two will be?" asked Bill.

"I need to ensure that the audience is actively engaged in the presentation. Leaving that obvious point out will allow an opportunity for the HR director and CFO to provide the cost of those additional employees, thus making them participants in solving the problem and increasing their ownership on the final decision."

"You're not going to provide them with more information on the interactive awareness automated solution?" Paula asked.

"These are seniors, if they have questions, they'll ask, and it provides another chance for them to interact," Dan said, "Right Sophie?"

"Correct!" Sophie responded, "Give us another example."

"We don't have procedures for what we are to do if we have a major system failure, caused by nature, loss of the facility, hacker, or malicious code attacks.

"The solution here is simple. We can have the task group, with some technical support from the security consultants, conduct a review of the problem and provide recommendations to management in a month; cost $10,000."

"That was short and sweet, very good. Do you have another?" asked Sophie.

"Weak passwords are a major vulnerability and there are many options.

"The first is a new procedure and change in policy. The procedure is that the IT department personnel conduct frequent reviews of the system's password files for weak passwords. By using a hacker tool called 'cracker', we identify users that are using weak passwords. If we find someone, we call them to our office, explain what we found and educate them on what a good password looks like. The change in policy is: If someone is found using a weak password twice, the CIO will explain it to them, and the third time, they visit the Director of Human Relations for disciplinary action."

"Senior management support always helps," Paula commented.

"This is a good check, but that does not eliminate the problem of people writing them on sticky notes, so we are recommending that we procure an authentication token for each employee to carry on their ID badge chain. The token provides the employee with a **dynamic** or **one-time password** each time they login to the system."

"**Dynamic password**?" asked Bill.

"That means that the password is different each time that the employee logs into the system. That way if they wrote it down or someone collected the password, the system would not accept it as valid during the next login.

With approximately 600 people on the system, the cost would be between $20,000 and $30,000.

There is an added advantage to this solution: increased security awareness. We accomplish this by requiring our employees to clip it to the employee badges that they have on the lanyard around their neck to provide a constant visual reminder of the need for security."

"Good example of increased return-on-investment, we call it an ROI justification," Bill said.

"I am also going to use flattery to further the case. I plan on recommending that the senior management receive the first tokens. That way management can demonstrate that they actively support the organization's IT security program and all the employees will be standing in line to get their tokens."

"Excellent!" Bill commented.

"Yes, you have done very well," Sophie said, "It sounds like you know the problems and your audience, are providing them options, have justified your recommendations, are confident, and in charge. Now we'll see if you walk away with the pot."

"Wish me luck."

"You don't need luck. You have a strategy," responded Bill.

"And because of that our bets are on you. Right?" Paula asked.

"Right!" Bill and Sophie responded in unison.

SCOREPAD

No one can sell your solutions better than <u>YOU.</u>

Give the credit to others.

Provide options and recommendations.

Provide opportunities for the participants to get involved by leaving obvious questions for them to ask.

Sixth Game Night

The Chips

The Chips

As Dan walked through the door, everyone was on the edge of their seats waiting to hear the results of his presentation.

"First and foremost," he began, "thank you all for your dedicated and unwavering support helping me with this challenging opportunity."

"Cut the flattery and tell us what happened!" said Bill.

"They supported all of my recommendations. My boss has accepted the residual risk. I got an increased budget. I know how to sell my ideas to management and how to influence future funding, and I have an in depth understanding of my IT system, which allows me to respond more efficiently to problems."

"That's great. Anything else?" asked Sophie.

"The seniors were very impressed with how I explained the security issues and solutions and related them to our business goals. They were so impressed that they are promoting me to the position of Chief Security Officer."

"Congratulations!" they all shouted.

"I guess we know who is in the chips now."

"Drinks are on me!" Dan exclaimed.

SCOREPAD

A RISK ASSESSMENT IS A TOTAL
SECURITY REVIEW BASED ON THE
MISSION AND BUSINESS.

APPROVING WHAT IS AN
" ACCEPTABLE RISK " IS A
MANAGEMENT DECISION, NOT A
TECHNICAL DECISION.

RISK DECISIONS ARE MADE BY
THOSE WITH OPERATIONAL, POLICY,
POLITICAL, AND FINANCIAL
AUTHORITY.

RISK IS A BALANCE OF BUSINESS
AND SECURITY REQUIREMENTS.

KEY POINTS

CONFRONTING SOMETHING NEW – PAGE 29

-Manage it, don't avoid it.

-Understand the unknowns.

-Establish a strategy.

-Take charge.

DISCOVERING THE OBJECTIVES – PAGE 35

-Identify the players and their motivations.

-Learn the processes and the timing of the key actions.

-Luck is a loser's crutch. Research is a winner's edge.

KNOWING A SECURITY ASSESSMENT – PAGE 52

Certification Report

-Technical review by experts

-Threats, vulnerabilities and countermeasures

-Residual risks

-Recommendations

Accreditation

-Operational and/or political decision by management

-Accept residual risk

-Interim conditional use

Understanding Assessment Concepts – Page 61

-Certification is a technical evaluation of the IT system's security.

-Accreditation is management's operational and political decision to accept the residual risk.

-When there are multiple standards, there are no standards.

-Flexibility provides options. Use it to your advantage.

Finding Good Security Solutions – Page 71

-Understand the rules, best practices, and regulations.

-Remember that they are guidelines, not checklists.

-Follow the prudent man rule: due care and due diligence.

-Do what is practical and logical for your situation.

Managing a Security Assessment – Page 79

-Know all players and their motivations.

-Know who gives the ultimate approval.

-Take charge of the effort.

Taking Risks – Page 89

-100% security is not affordable.

-Acceptable Risk is accepting Residual Risk.

-The Accreditation Authority accepts the Residual Risk.

-Develop a strategy.

Basing Security on Business Needs – Page 99

-IT Security is based on business needs first.

-Involve the majority of the players to gain their awareness and ownership.

-Sell management on security using business logic.

Gaining Support – Page 103

-Know the "Golden Rule:"
"He who has the Gold, makes the Rules."

-Know how to influence the gold.

-Know the people, goals, processes, and timing.

-Use your judgement and flattery works.

Understanding Security Experts – Page 111

-Understanding the real system's needs helps set real priorities.

-Pictures really are worth a thousand words.

-Ask for specific references to verify facts.

-Wait as long as it takes to get an answer.

Using a Total Security Approach – Page 114

-Look at the entire environment and all potential security solutions.

-Sometimes physical, personnel, and procedural security solutions are better than the technical solutions.

-A system can have total security, but it can never be totally secure.

SELLING SECURITY – PAGE 117

-Sell using the security solutions value to the business.

-Provide the decision-makers with options.

-Base your recommendations on the decision-makers' motivations.

KNOWING YOUR BOSSES – PAGE 121

-No one likes surprises.

-Pre-educate to set key players' expectations.

-Keep presentations simple, let them ask questions.

-Note all questions and guidance provided by seniors.

INFLUENCING RESOURCES – PAGE 129

-Budget is about process, planning, timing, and justifications.

-Justifications are about player motivations and business goals.

-Ask players for their advice and guidance.

PROMOTING SOLUTIONS – PAGE 139

-No one can sell your solutions better than you.

-Give the credit to others.

-Provide options and recommendations.

-Provide opportunities for the participants to get involved by leaving obvious questions for them to ask.

THE MAIN POINTS – PAGE 145

-A risk assessment is a total security review based on the mission and business.

-Approving what is an "acceptable risk" is a management decision, not a technical decision.

-Risk decisions are made by those with operational, policy, political, and financial authority.

-Risk is a balance of business and security requirements.

AUTHORS

Jim Litchko and Al Payne are not only IT security professionals, they have also been executives, managers, business developers, speakers, and educators in commercial and government sectors.

Jim Litchko has thirty years of security experience, twenty years as a Naval Officer, five years at the National Security Agency (NSA), managed world-wide operational IT systems, conducted over 100 security assessments, and worked as a senior manager in the government and commercial industry. Since 1988, he has been an adjunct professor at Johns Hopkins University and taught courses at many professional security institutions. Jim is also a professional member of the National Speakers' Association and the author of *KNOW Your Life* and *KNOW IT Security*.

Al Payne has thirty years of IT experience including nine years in security. Al is a Certified Information Systems Security Professional (CISSP), has been an officer in the U.S. Marine Corps, business owner, executive, operational manager, strategic advisor for business, and is an entrepreneur whose business plans have secured millions in business capital.

Both are active members of the Federal Information Systems Security Education Association (FISSEA) and have instructed IT managers on how to conduct business-based security assessments and how to sell security to executives in the commercial and government sectors.

SPECIAL THANKS

KNOW Cyber Risk couldn't have been completed without the special help from friends and associates. The support and encouragement they provided was truly commendable. Thanks for the initial edit of the book by Erin Sexton and special thanks to Kristin Adolfson for the final edit, formatting, and publishing of *KNOW Cyber Risk*. Finally to our lovely brides, Jane and Susan, who provided us with the critical inputs on the many drafts and supported our hours, days, weeks, and months locked in our offices and on travel working to develop this book.

OTHER BOOKS BY AUTHOR JIM LITCHKO

KNOW IT Security – Secure IT Systems Casino Style

KNOW IT Security is a realistic story for CEOs, CFOs, CIOs, CSOs and their personnel who are looking for a basic introduction to IT security concepts, terms, and strategies. The reader is provided a:

- *low-tech* introduction to IT security threats and countermeasures, firewalls, encryption, intrusion detection systems, backups, etc.

- *business-based* strategies for assessing IT system security needs.

- *total security approach* to securing IT systems using technical, personnel, physical, and procedural security methods.

After reading **KNOW IT Security**, you will have a basic understanding of IT security that will allow you to ask knowledgeable questions, make better decisions, and have the confidence to learn more on this complex topic.

KNOW Your Life – By Organizing It!

Become more effective and efficient in managing and organizing your life while saving time, gaining control over demands, and increasing your confidence in handling crisis situations. ***KNOW Your Life*** condenses all your records and personal documents into one place and serves as a reference that quickly supports you, your partner, or your loved ones during everyday tasks or in times of crisis. You will gain the tools to organize your:

- ***Personal Identity***: birth certificates, passports, drivers licenses...
- ***Income:*** employment, retirement, social security...
- ***Finances:*** bank accounts, credit cards...
- ***Investments:*** stocks, bonds...
- ***Properties:*** house, timeshares, cars, boats...
- ***Insurance:*** life, property, car...
- ***Health:*** medial plans, hospitals, doctors...
- ***Wishes:*** wills, arrangements, notifications...

For more information on these books visit www.knowbookpublishing.com

QUICK ORDER FORM

Give the gift of *KNOW Cyber Risk* to colleagues, managers, or security professionals.

	QTY	TOTAL
KNOW Cyber Risk for $14.95 USD each	_____	$_____
KNOW IT Security for $14.95 USD each	_____	$_____
Sales tax: Maryland residents add 5% sales tax	**MD Tax**	$_____
Shipping costs: Include $3.75 USD shipping & handling for first book and $3.00 for each additional book.	**Shipping**	$_____
	TOTAL	$_____

❑ **YES!** I am interested in having James P. Litchko and Al Payne speak or give a seminar at my company, association, school, or organization. Please send me more information.

Please allow 3 weeks for delivery after publication.

Payment: Payment must accompany orders. Make check or money order payable to *Know Book Publishing*, or complete the following credit card information and sign:

Please charge my: ❑ VISA   ❑ MASTERCARD   ❑ AMERICAN EXPRESS

BILLING INFORMATION

Name:_____

Organization:_____

Address: _____

City/State/Zip:_____

Phone: _____

Card Number:_____

Exp. Date:_____

SHIPPING ADDRESS ❑ same as billing

Name:_____

Address Line1:_____

Address Line2:_____

City/State/Zip:_____

E-mail: _____

Name On Card:_____

Signature: _____

Fax orders: 240-363-0231. Send this completed form. Credit card orders only.

Web orders: Visit http://www.knowbookpublishing.com to order via the Internet.

Postal orders: Mail this completed form to: Know Book Publishing
P.O. Box G
Kensington, MD. 20895